fit

PRINCETON UNIVERSITY PRESS   PRINCETON AND OXFORD

fit

an architect's manifesto

robert geddes

Published by Princeton University Press,
41 William Street, Princeton, New Jersey 08540
In the United Kingdom: Princeton University Press, 6
Oxford Street, Woodstock, Oxfordshire OX20 1TW
press.princeton.edu

An earlier version of portions of this book appeared
as "The Forest Edge," *Architectural Design Profile*
(London: Architectural Design, 1982).

Excerpt from "Baby, It's Cold Outside,"
by Frank Loesser
© 1948 (renewed) FRANK MUSIC CORP.
All rights reserved
Reprinted by Permission of Hal Leonard Corporation

Library of Congress Cataloging-in-Publication Data
Geddes, Robert.
Fit : an architect's manifesto / Robert Geddes.
pages cm
Includes bibliographical references and index.
ISBN 978-0-691-15575-3 (pbk. : alk. paper)
1. Architecture—Philosophy. I. Title.
NA2500.G394 2012
720.1—dc23
2012014059

British Library Cataloging-in-Publication Data is available
This book has been composed in Helvetica Neue
and Sabon
Printed on acid-free paper. ∞
Printed in the United States of America
1 3 5 7 9 10 8 6 4 2

To Evelyn

In *From a Cause to a Style*,[1] Nathan Glazer expressed the "growing disenchantment of an early enthusiast of modernism in architecture and planning—and who when young is not?—with the failures of modernist architects and planners in dealing with contemporary urban life." Why so? Because "modernism evolved into something intended to surprise, to astound, to disorient, perhaps to amuse. It was not an architecture for ordinary life, and ordinary life has fled from it."[2]

Ouch. That hurts.

According to legend, a psychologist at a conference once said that the problem with architects is that "they always take things personally." Immediately, an architect in the back row jumped up and shouted, "I do not." That protester could have been me.

This book is my response to Nathan Glazer's remorse.

contents

1A. Ambrogio Lorenzetti, *Good Government in the City* (1338–
1340), detail, fresco on wall of Council Room in Palazzo
Pubblico, Siena, Italy. The Bridgeman Art Library

2. The underground Apple Store on
Avenue, New York, is entered thro
transparent glass cube at the cent
plaza. The thirty-two-foot cube an

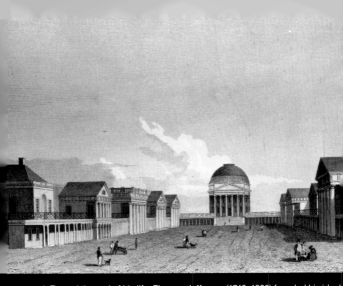

4. Toward the end of his life, Thomas Jefferson (1743–1826) founded his ideal

Usonia 1 in Madison, Wisconsin, was the first in Frank Lloyd Wright's brilliant series of affordable houses, designed for families throughout agrarian America ("Usonia" was Wright's name for the "United States of North America"). Wright connected architecture with its setting in nature, from the prairie to the wilderness. His architectural forms were aimed at human experience—the family's hearth at the core of the house, the open plan of the living areas, the functional and visual transparency with the landscape. Usonia 1, designed by architect Frank Lloyd Wright (1936–1937). © 2012 Frank Lloyd Wright Foundation, Scottsdale, AZ / Artists Rights Society (ARS), NY / Art Resource, NY.

6. The New York Public Library is a people's palace. It fits splendidly between a street and a green park; the architectural expression comes from the design principles of the École des Beaux-Arts. Inside is a monumental reading room; the library's function is the education and intellectual development of all citizens. As a physical form, the library is a delight from the City Beautiful movement; as a social form, it is a legacy from the Progressive Era. New York Public Library, designed by architects Carrère and Hastings (1897–1911).

New York's Rockefeller Center is a triumph of private development, a workplace for thousands of people. It is also an architectural triumph: a dynamic composition of low and high buildings, combining Beaux-Arts symmetry with modernist verticality; it is a remarkable group plan. At street level, all buildings open directly onto sidewalks; identical low pavilions create civic places between them: the Channel Gardens slope gently to a sunken plaza, ice rink, and golden Prometheus fountain. Rockefeller Center, New York, designed by Rockefeller Center Associated Architects: Reinhard and Hofmeister; Hood, Godley and Foulihoux; Corbett, Harrison and MacMurray (1931–1939)

Civic Form: Populism / Monumentalism

8A. Pike Place is Seattle's public market for farmers and crafters—its sign proudly proclaims, "Meet the Producer." Originally built in 1907, it was under threat of demolition, rescued, and reimagined by civic activists in the 1960s, and continues to evolve as a vibrant, diverse neighborhood. Pike Place, civic design by architect Victor Steinbrueck and Friends of the Market (1963–). Photo © David Kadlubowski / DIT / Corbis

8B. Millennium Park began with Daniel Burnham's monumental plan for Chicago and the lakefront; it was completed with Frank Gehry's ode to joy—a stainless-steel band shell with a Great Lawn and acoustic trellis for the multitude. Millennium Park, Jay Pritzker Music Pavilion, designed by architect Frank Gehry (1999–2004). Jay Pritzher Pavilion on Beethoven's 9th Symphony Day, TonyTheTiger

illustrations

acknowledgments

To my wife, Evelyn, my son, David, and my daughter, Ann, with thanks for spirited conversations over so many decades.

To my mentors in academic life, Robert F. Goheen, president of Princeton University; Deans Joseph Hudnut at Harvard University and G. Holmes Perkins at the University of Pennsylvania; and to my partners in professional life, Melvin Brecher, George Qualls, and Warren Cunningham.

To the editors and staff of the Princeton University Press, with thanks for their creative skills and collegial spirit: the director, Peter Dougherty; Lauren Lepow, copyeditor; Julia Livingston, editorial staff; Jason Alejandro, designer; Bob Bettendorf, copywriter; Tom Broughton-Willett, freelance indexer; Neil Litt, production director; and many others around the coffee machine.

To readers of the work at various points in its development: John Morris Dixon, Robert Freidin, Alan Chimacoff, Hamilton Ross, Urs Gauchat, and Alan Ryan.

To the many colleagues who joined me for lunch while the book was under way, including Stan Allen, Christine Boyer, Marvin Bressler, Alan Chimacoff, Esther da Costa Meyer, Peter Dougherty, Robert Freidin, Mario Gandelsonas, Oleg Grabar, Robert Gutman, Azel Kilian, Donald Light, Cary Liu, Neil Litt, Michael Mostoller, Chuck Myers, Anson Rabinbach, Alan Ryan, P. Adams Sitney, Stanley Stein, Heinrich von Staden, and Sarah Whiting.

Introduction

Designing

We are all designers.

Every day, we organize things to accomplish goals, from the shape of the table for a peace conference to the strategic development program for a business. Perhaps, like Winston Churchill, we might even be called the "architect of victory."

Designing means creating, organizing, placing, setting things to achieve a purpose. Working as designers, we make things fit together.

> *Everyone designs who devises courses of action aimed at changing existing situations into preferred ones.*
>
> —HERBERT A. SIMON, ECONOMIST[3]

Designing differs fundamentally from both art and science. An artist seeks feeling and expression, and a scientist seeks knowledge and explanation; but neither works to achieve a predetermined, known, objective, defined purpose. By contrast, a designer is always driven by purpose. Designing—as both a process and a product—is always connected to something outside itself.

Environments

Why do we design where we live and work? Why do we not just live in nature, or in chaos, or in ad hoc environments?

We need an **understandable** environment. We need to know where we are, where we have come from, and where we are heading. We need to be able to understand the place around us—its organization and meaning. We need a sense of place.

We need an **operational** environment. We need a functional place that protects us in our surroundings, enables us to carry out the tasks of our lives. We need places that work for us, providing us with farms for agricultural production, factories and cities for economic production, fortresses for military protection, sports grounds for pleasure, churches and mosques and temples for religious rituals.

We need an **ethical** environment, because what we build is such a powerful agent of change in both nature and society. The built environment can be a destroyer of resources and a threat to biological species, including our own. At its best, it can provide productive and sustainable environments. But ethical questions always arise: for whom do we build, and with what consequences?

We need an **aesthetic** environment that delights our senses with light and color, the smooth and the rough, the warm and the cool, the vibrant and the still. We need places where we experience order and complexity, unity and diversity, harmony and dissonance, proportion and rhythm. We want to experience beauty and the promise of happiness.

> *For it is still the case that no one lives in the world in general. Everybody, even the exiled, the drifting, the diasporic, or the perpetually moving, lives in some confined and limited stretch of it—"the world around here."*

> —CLIFFORD GEERTZ, ANTHROPOLOGIST[4]

By necessity, we live in buildings.
By choice, we live in architecture.

Build we must, to protect and shelter ourselves. To live and work together, we build buildings. Buildings are our sustaining mechanisms.

Simultaneously, we signal who we are, where we are, what we are doing. We express ourselves, our memories, our social institutions, our places—in architecture.

Architecture in Our Times

Historians tell us that we are in the midst of an "age of fracture," living in "architecture's evil empire." Out of despair, they are crying for help:

> But then in the last quarter of the century, through more and more domains of social thought and argument, the terms that had dominated post–World War II intellectual life began to fracture. One heard less about society, history, and power and more about individuals, contingency, and choice. . . . History was said to accelerate into a multitude of almost instantaneously accessible possibilities. . . . In the last quarter of the century, the dominant tendency of the age was toward disaggregation.
>
> —Daniel Rodgers, social historian[5]
>
> Where architecture in previous eras was like the continuous text of a book, with foreground and background passages

in mutual support, today's architectural
culture has fragmented itself into a maze
of disjointed quotations, some individually
memorable but collectively disorienting. . . .
Something has to be done to begin joining
up the pieces—but what?

—MILES GLENDINNING, ARCHITECTURAL
HISTORIAN[6]

"Something has to be done to begin joining up the pieces—but what?"

We need a more inclusive architecture.

It must fit the here and now.
It must be fit for future possibilities.

It must fit.

What does it mean, "fit the here and now"?
It is the opposite of "architecture for its own
sake." It is engaged with social and environmental conditions. It is profoundly political. It
is connected to arts and humanities. It works
with sciences and technologies. It means
architecture that is fit for the purpose and fit
for the place.

What does it mean, "be fit for future
possibilities"? Some humility is needed here,

because we do not know the future, now; but we can think, design, build, and live with it in mind. That would be a profound step toward "inclusive architecture." Ask, what was here before, and what might follow us? How should we change, and how should we grow?

We need a better way to evaluate architecture. It should replace the modernists' "Form follows function" and the always fashionable "What does it look like?" It should be widely debated by architects and clients, users of buildings, community leaders, and makers of public policies and plans. It should be focused, seemingly obvious but actually unlimited in its implications and connections. It should be powerful—like the physicians' Hippocratic oath, "Do no harm." How should we frame the "oath of architecture"?

Architecture should embrace fitness—order and organization, growth and form. The "oath of architecture" should be loud and clear: make it fit.

Fit

The architect's task is to formulate things that fit.

Fit the purpose.
Fit the place.
Fit for future possibilities.

> Leon Battista Alberti (1404–1472)
> Italy: Renaissance
>
> *To every Member therefore ought to be allotted its fit place and proper situation.*

> Karl Friedrich Schinkel (1781–1841)
> Germany: Neoclassical
>
> *Architecture is the combination of various materials into a unit bound together by suitability to purpose. . . . it is clearly manifest that fitness is the fundamental principle of Architecture.*

> August Welby Pugin (1812–1852)
> England: Gothic Revival
>
> *The great test of architectural beauty is the fitness of the design for the purpose intended.*

> Christopher Alexander (b. 1936)
> England / United States: Modern
>
> *[E]very design problem begins with an effort to achieve fitness between two entities: the form and its context. The form is the solution to the problem; the context defines the problem.*

Architecture for Architecture's Sake?

Dear Theo,

Will life never treat me decently? I am wracked by despair! My head is pounding! Mrs. Sol Schwimmer is suing me because I made her bridge as I felt it and not to fit her ridiculous mouth! That's right! . . . I decided her bridge should be enormous and billowing, with wild, explosive teeth flaring up in every direction like fire! Now she is upset because it won't fit in her mouth! She is so bourgeois and stupid, I want to smash her! I tried forcing the false plate in but it sticks out like a star burst chandelier. Still, I find it beautiful. She claims she can't chew! What do I care whether she can chew or not! Theo, I can't go on like this much longer! . . .

Vincent

—Woody Allen[7]

Architects sometimes insist that what they do serves no external purpose, that it is an end in itself, to be understood purely on its own terms. Like "art for art's sake," could there be "architecture for architecture's sake"? Fascination with the idea of "autonomous architecture" comes from an intellectual tradition with some respectable sources, such as the philosopher Immanuel Kant. When Kant divided human capability into three categories—cognitive knowledge, moral conscience, and aesthetic sensibility—he opened the door to "autonomous" conditions, in which the true, the good, and the beautiful are separated from each other. Thus writer and critic Théophile Gautier could claim that aesthetics has nothing to do with usefulness: "Only those things that are altogether useless can be truly beautiful: anything that is useful is ugly."[8] Writer Oscar Wilde could claim that art had nothing to do with an ethical life: "No artist has ethical sympathies. An ethical sympathy is an unpardonable mannerism of style."[9] And the painter Clive Bell could claim that "we need bring with us nothing but a sense of form, color, and a knowledge of three-dimensional space."[10]

For some architects, "autonomy" seems irresistible. Here, for example, is a contemporary architect's confession: "Architecture is made by architects for themselves. . . . My best work is without purpose."[11] This narcissistic statement may be just a provocative gesture . . . but it also may be true. How or why a work was initially imagined is not crucial—if it does fit.

"Something has to be done to begin joining up the pieces—but what?"

We need a renewed sense that architecture must be designed to make things fit.

The Origin of Architecture Is Nature

Experiencing Nature: Light

We live in sunlight and shadow, daylight and
darkness. We experience the annual light
cycle of nature—the four seasons of summer,
fall, winter, and spring—and the daily light
cycle, between sunrise and sunset. Unlike the
pull of gravity, which remains constant, the
light of nature is always changing.

> *In the beginning God created the heaven and*
> *the earth.*
> *And the earth was without form, and void;*
> *And darkness was upon the face of the deep.*
> *And God said, Let there be light: and there was*
> *light.*
>
> —Book of Genesis

Nowadays, we can create artificial light,
distribute it, and use it whenever and wherever we wish. By contrast, our ancestors had

natural light from only two sources: from the heavens (sunlight, moonlight, and starlight, and sometimes lightning), and from fire on earth.

All species must deal with sunlight, because photosynthesis (the process that converts sunlight to energy) is a basis of life on earth. "It is why we need the sun and why we must make our own light when the sun is gone. . . . illumination, the human creation of light, comforts us."[12]

> *There will also be natural propriety in using an eastern light for bedrooms and libraries, a western light in winter for baths and winter apartments, and a northern light for picture galleries and other places in which a steady light is needed; for that quarter of the sky grows neither light nor dark with the course of the sun, but remains steady and unshifting all day long.*
>
> —MARCUS VITRUVIUS POLLIO, *DE ARCHITECTURA*, BK. 1, CHAP. 2: "THE FUNDAMENTAL PRINCIPLES OF ARCHITECTURE"

Only our species captures, controls, and uses fire. We have constructed environments to protect ourselves from rampant fire and excessive sunlight; and we also have built to capture, control, and use both of our dominant sources of light—fire and sunlight.

Historians tell us that through the ages our ancestors enjoyed natural light for hunting, fishing, and working the soil during the day, but nightfall brought terror. In medieval Europe, people prepared for darkness as a ship's crew prepares for a storm.

Inside, the comfort of light and heat came from the fire of a hearth. Buildings came to be known by the number of their hearths, as boats are recognized by the number of their sails.

Throughout human history, fire was essential for making artificial light: candles (burning animal fat, beeswax, or paraffin), oil lanterns (burning oil from plants or animals), gas lamps (burning petroleum or natural gas), and torches (burning anything that flames). Unlike the fixed location of a hearth, candles and lanterns could be carried around, to light the way. They were portable light for places and processions.

Industrial society invented continuous light, available anywhere, anytime, on demand. In an agrarian society like George Washington's, there was little need for round-the-clock artificial light because most people (more than nine out of ten) were occupied producing food—in natural light. By contrast, today, we have light whenever and wherever we want it.

We design light according to how we see, both close-up and far away. For example, if we want to sew on a button (requiring close vision) and also look at people across the room (requiring far vision), we need two different kinds of light: "task" lighting for the space close to us, and "ambient" lighting for the overall space surrounding us.

We are drawn to light according to its source: we sit at home by the window in sunlight, and we gather under a skylight, in hotel lobbies, in shopping malls, in the center of sacred and civic places.

We use light according to its place. At home, we use a porch light, a hall light, a kitchen light. At work, we use a desk light, an exit light. In theaters, we use houselights and stage lights.

We change light according to the occasion: at home, we dim the lights when putting children to bed; at public rallies, we turn on spotlights; and in church, we light the altar candles.

To understand where we are, how we can move from place to place, we use light as a navigational compass. The animal mind (including ours) uses sunlight—the sunrise in the east and the sunset in the west—to create cardinal directions (north, south, east, west). These four directions crisscross to create gridiron networks. Animal architects use sunlight grids to plan their shelters, build networks of paths (avenues), form their bowers (neighborhoods) and cities. Naturally, we have Sunrise Highway on Long Island (east) and Sunset Boulevard in Hollywood (west).

Experiencing Nature: Gravity

> *The Universal Law of Gravitation: two particles attract each other with forces directly proportional to the product of their masses divided by the square of the distance between them.*
>
> —ISAAC NEWTON, PRINCIPIA

Gravity is not random. On earth, the force of gravity is always with us, everywhere. We experience its pull on our bodies when we stand up, when we jump, and when we hold something up.

We enjoy talking about our personal experiences of gravity. We use it in metaphors to express our feelings—"I jumped for joy" or "my heart sank." We also invoke it in public conversations—the "heavy responsibility of the president" and "the gravity of the situation." On a happier note, when looking at architecture, we may speak of arches "leaping" and towers "soaring."

The gravitational force that acts on our bodies also acts on our buildings. No surprise, then, that we delight in airy dynamic structures (like the Eiffel Tower), and also admire solid stable structures (like the Egyptian pyramids). Although they look very different from each other, they gain their stability by using the same geometric form—a triangle. The bottom of the triangle is the "ground" in nature and the "floor" in architecture.

Unlike light and heat, which can work in all directions, gravity works in only one way—down. Gravity gives us a vertical line, and we imagine its mate, a horizontal plane.

Because we live with natural gravity on a planet shaped like a sphere, verticals point inward toward the center of the earth, and horizontals bend around it. Absolute verticals and absolute horizontals do not exist in nature, but at the human scale, we live as if they did exist—and we express them in architecture, the vertical column and the horizontal beam.

Together, the column and beam create a three-dimensional grid framework. It has profound meanings in architecture. It works as an organizational form for our sense of place, and as a structural form to deal with forces of gravity.

But, to deal with gravity, there are many other possibilities. We delight in vaults that soar upward across space, like the Pantheon in Rome, the medieval cathedrals in France, the railway terminal sheds in London, the Opera House in Sydney Harbour. We also delight in suspension structures that take their form—by necessity, not by choice—in response to the downward pull of gravity.

Gravity's downward pull creates what is called a "catenary" curve. It is a beautiful form, most often seen when a structure is in tension, such as a steel cable with a downward sloping curve: or in compression, such as a concrete dome with an upward curve. Most domes over rotundas, like that of the Pantheon in Rome or the Capitol building in Washington, do not look like an upside-down catenary, inside or outside; they look more like a sphere, a simpler geometry. The observer's eye and mind may not be more satisfied, but the builder has an easier task.

Static stability or dynamic equilibrium? All architectural history hangs in the balance, so to speak. The question still attracts attention—the *New York Times* recently noted with some delight that "[a] dry stone wall is a wall built without mortar," so that, unlike the composition of a mortared wall, "only two things hold a dry stone wall together: gravity and friction."[13]

In the beginning was the wall; the column grew free of the wall, and the Classical language of architecture was born. With its columns and beams, walls and vaults, the static stability of Classical structures evolved, during the medieval era, into the dynamic equilibrium of ribbed vaults and buttresses of Gothic construction. In the modern era, the Classical stability of Louis Sullivan's Wainwright Building, in St. Louis, and Mies van der Rohe's Seagram Building, in New York, contrasts with the dynamic balancing act of Frank Lloyd Wright's cantilevered house over a waterfall, and Frank Gehry's metal sails billowing over a museum, which are daring, risk-taking contests with gravity, a realization of Icarus's dream of flight.

And our modern dream of flight aspires even higher. If we really want to live in outer space, we will need to substitute an artificial gravity for natural gravity. Otherwise, the long-term experience of weightlessness would have terrible consequences for us, as human animals. Our body fluids would shift toward the head; the brain would respond to the increase in fluid by activating the excretory mechanisms, leading to dehydration; our automatic regulatory systems would not work normally, causing changes in our heart size and output; our muscles would atrophy owing to lack of use; we would experience bone damage, loss of red blood cells, loss of weight, extreme flatulence, degraded senses of smell and taste, changes in body size, and facial distortions. Not a pretty picture.

If we succeed in creating livable environments in outer space, perhaps artificial gravity will come to be as commonplace in our experience as artificial heat and artificial light.

Meanwhile, back on Earth, understanding artificial gravity gives us a better understanding of how to live every day with natural gravity. Our bodies cannot survive without gravity; and our buildings must know how to perform with it. Our survival depends on it.

Experiencing Nature: Landscapes

Nature is the place where buildings and landscapes and cities are built—and it is also a source of their ideas and images.

The beginning of architecture was Adam's primitive hut in paradise, according to the eighteenth-century architectural theorist

Marc-Antoine Laugier. In his *Essai sur l'architecture*,[14] the frontispiece shows a seated Muse pointing to a hut made of four trees that serve as wood columns, at the edge of a forest.

Another interpretation of Laugier's frontispiece is that the Muse is directing our attention not only to the building as a reconstructed forest, but also to the edge of the forest itself. She indicates that where the woodlands and grasslands meet is the ideal landscape for humankind.

We live our everyday lives in landscapes. We experience nature in three kinds of landscapes:

> the wild landscapes of forests and mountains;
> the pastoral landscapes of pasturelands and
>   farmlands; and
> the urban landscapes of cities and metropolitan
>   regions.

When we live in a landscape, we are transforming nature into a habitat. As a place for living, a landscape is like a building: it is an artifact of its culture and society. Obviously, our cities are constructed landscapes; but so are our pastoral landscapes, which transform nature into working farms. Even our wilderness landscapes exist today only because of our decisions to preserve them.

The three landscapes—the wild, the pastoral, the urban—conflict deeply with each other when, for example, agrarian landscapes are carved out of the wilderness, or urban landscapes spread into farmlands. Conflicts over landscapes arise from both pragmatic necessities and symbolic associations. Different ideals build different landscapes.

In the history of ideas in America, architecture's preeminent domain—the city—has often been denigrated by intellectuals, poets, and painters. They tended to value the relationship between man and the wild landscape, or man and the pastoral landscape, but not man and the urban landscape.

Nineteenth-century American paintings reflected, on the one hand, a sense of the incredible marvel of the wilderness and, on the other, a perception of the delights of pastoral life and the dream of Arcadia. Even the new symbol of technology, power, and progress—the railroad—was portrayed both in the setting of a pastoral landscape (George Inness's *The Lackawanna Valley*) and in a wilderness (Thomas Prichard Rossiter's *Opening of the Wilderness*). The divergent ideals of landscape expressed by the painters were also articulated in the history of ideas in America by, among others, Henry David Thoreau and Thomas Jefferson.

Wilderness Landscapes

Thoreau saw man as virtuous only when in direct contact with the wilderness landscape. He rejected society, in both its agrarian and its urban forms. He said, "I wish to speak a word for Nature, for absolute Freedom and Wildness . . . to regard man as an inhabitant, or a part and parcel of Nature, rather than a member of society."[15]

Americans have used two strategies to bring about the direct connection between man and the wilderness landscape. One strategy requires conservation and preservation. For example, following the 1964 Wilderness Act, some fifteen million acres have been placed under the Wilderness Preservation System in units ranging from more than a million to only six acres. The other strategy has been the deliberate creation of facsimiles of wilderness landscapes, conceived under the influence of the romantic movement with its ideal of the natural life.

The ideal of romanticism first appeared in America as a built environment in new cemeteries, such as Mount Auburn in Cambridge, Massachusetts (1831), and Laurel Hill near Philadelphia (1835). Later, the image of the ideal romantic landscape appeared in the new designs for suburbs, such as Llewellyn Park

(1857) outside Newark, New Jersey. These suburbs were a reaction against the urban landscape; their influence persists in suburbs built today. The characteristics of both the new cemeteries and the romantic suburbs were curving streets, irregular positioning of plants and trees, and the placement of buildings in an architectural relationship not to each other or a street, but to trees and meadows.

Thoreau's ideas of man and wilderness landscape suggest possibilities for architecture. One is the notion of setting a man-made object in an apparently untouched natural landscape—for example, the glass-and-steel Farnsworth House outside Chicago, designed by Mies van der Rohe (1945–1951). Another approach seeks to eliminate boundaries between the building interior and the landscape exterior. Both relationships with the wilderness landscape are evident in the design of Frank Lloyd Wright's Fallingwater, a house set in a forest (1936–1939). The cantilevered front of the house is hung over rocks, while the back of the house is embedded within them.

The necessity of sustainability, expressed in the ecological and conservationist movements, has given new impetus to Thoreau's concept of the wilderness landscape. But these political movements do not actually propose that society should live in the wild. Indeed, since the wilderness cannot support even visitors in any great number, it cannot be an ecologically valid setting for buildings and cities.

Pastoral Landscapes

Unlike Thoreau, who saw virtue in direct contact between man and wilderness, Jefferson believed in creating a pastoral landscape that would foster political virtue in its inhabitants. He argued that "[t]hose who labor in the earth are the chosen people of God, if ever he had a chosen people, whose breasts he has made his peculiar deposit for substantial and genuine virtue."[16]

Jefferson's influence on the built environment came about intellectually, through his emphasis on the pastoral as the ideal landscape, and pragmatically, through his advocacy of the grid, on a national scale in his Public Land Survey System of 1785. The grid created by the survey was a rational, geometric form for a pastoral landscape. It was the opposite of the cluster pattern of medieval landscapes, because there were no centers. It was democratic and egalitarian, because all space within it was equal. The ideal, structured, continuous pattern surcharged Jefferson's ideals and ideas on the emerging continental nation.

The idea of the grid was not new to America. The original plans for New Haven (1638) and Philadelphia (1683) had been laid out on a grid. Jefferson used a grid for his own ideal city, Jeffersonville, and advocated it for new cities, such as the capital at Washington. As Americans moved west, their new cities were laid out as a mosaic of grids. Our subsequent urban experience has proved Jefferson right when he argued for the grid in terms of its egalitarian and pragmatic qualities.

Jefferson's conception of the proper relationship between intellectual ideas and buildings and landscape can best be seen at the Academical Village (1819–1825) for the University of Virginia (plate 4), which he designed following his presidency of the United States. The university's architectural form has linear colonnades (the building equivalent of a forest) framing a central lawn (the landscape equivalent of a grassland).

Jefferson also applied his ideas for buildings and landscapes at a small scale, in the house he built for himself at Monticello in Virginia. The house is set at the edge of a green clearing, surrounded by a walk along the edge of the forest.

In the twentieth century, from time to time, Jefferson's and Thoreau's ideals were knowingly embraced by architects. Frank Lloyd Wright is a case in point. As I've described, in placing Fallingwater within a Pennsylvania forest, Wright brought a house—and a family—into close contact with a wilderness landscape, in accordance with Thoreau's ideal. Meanwhile, Wright's designs for modest Usonian houses (named for the "United States of North America") show his devotion to Jefferson's pastoralism.

The typical Usonian house had a modular grid to compose both the landscape and the building (plate 5). The landscape consisted of lawns, arbors and gardens, and shade trees—essentially, a model of the Jeffersonian ideal for a pastoral America.

From the beginning of American conquest of the frontier wilderness, the dominant image of the good and beautiful landscape was distinctly pastoral, in the mainstream of Western classical culture since Virgil. The agrarian landscape was preferred because it supported a better political, social community.[17] The pastoral ideal, according to the historian Leo Marx, "has been used to define the meaning of America ever since the age of discovery, and it has not yet lost its hold upon the native imagination."[18] Pastoralism is more than a political economy; it is a collection of images about the world. The heart of pastoralism, as a way of life, is the freedom to hold discourse, to think, to make music and love in an ideal, ordered landscape.

Urban Landscapes

In colonial America, the layout of new towns and cities reflected their European roots. Some had irregular patterns of streets and buildings, resembling the organic growth pattern of medieval cities. But others were like Renaissance cities, with rectilinear streets and squares in a geometric plan.

New York shows both types of urban landscapes. At the southern end of Manhattan Island below Wall Street (named for a defensive wall built in 1653), buildings were set along irregular streets in a medieval pattern. As the settlement grew northward, the Dutch architecture with steep roofs and sharp gables, characteristic of the original settlement below Wall Street, gave way to calmer Renaissance styles popular in England. Just as the architectural style changed, so did the design of the new landscape change from the medieval to the Renaissance style. By the end of the eighteenth century, as the city grew northward, geometric patterns were laid upon the irregular land ("Manhattan" means hilly island in the Native American Algonquian language). In 1811, the commissioners' official map laid out a gridiron pattern for the city's future growth and form.

The gridiron was not a new idea. It had been the formal structure of ancient Roman cities and was later used in medieval Europe as the model for new towns, in contrast to the inherited irregular growth pattern. In Renaissance Europe, the geometric grid dominated the urban landscape. Geometry—an abstract creation of the human mind—was seen as a utopian ideal (see plate 1B). It was expressed in paintings through perspective views of rooms and landscapes, and it was achieved in cities by straight streets, uniform buildings along the street walls, square corners, and linear vistas. Gridirons were built as extensions to old cities and as structural frameworks for new cities.

Some new cities in America were built according to the Renaissance ideal for the orderly design of space. Philadelphia, for example, had a geometric plan characterized by the two essential elements of urban landscapes—streets and squares. The gridiron was subdivided by wide streets (on the north-south and east-west axes) creating four equal quadrants. Intentional open spaces—public squares—were laid out, one at the center, and one in each of the four quadrants. The gridiron, the pattern of streets and squares, was a spatial system for an urban landscape; ever since its founding, it has been the armature for growth and form of Philadelphia's center city.

From the outset, Philadelphia was conceived as a city-region. New settlers bought a land package consisting of outlying rural acreage and a center city building lot. For his future metropolis, William Penn proposed "to settle the figure of the town so as that the streets hereafter may be uniform down to the water from the country bounds."[19] Following Penn's instructions for the creation of a "Greene Country Towne," Philadelphia's center city gridiron was built between two riverbanks in a forest wilderness, Pennsylvania. Penn's conception of the city included connection with the countryside.

The connection of city and countryside also engaged the mind and imagination of Frederick Law Olmsted. As a landscape architect, driven by social and political ideals, Olmsted created some of our best urban landscapes: Central Park in Manhattan and Prospect Park in Brooklyn, greenswards in the midst of the metropolis; the Fenway in Boston, a necklace of green parks; and urban boulevards such as Commonwealth Avenue in Back Bay, Boston. Olmsted also crafted the landscape form of settlements outside of the central city. In Riverside, near Chicago, Olmsted created the new model of a suburb—curving streets, irregular land and plantings, naturalistic in the tradition of an English landscape garden.

The Forest Edge Ecology

Thoreau, Jefferson, and Olmsted were concerned with the form of our civilization, and with the influence upon it of the proper relationship of man and nature. The Jeffersonian pastoral ideal has been most widely adopted; his national survey has almost universally influenced the organization of our countrysides and the structure of our cities. In spite of a deep-rooted fascination with wilderness, our ideal image of "greenery" is an agrarian landscape.

From the scientific viewpoint, Jefferson's ideal is supported by natural history. Ecologists studied the ecosystems of the world and classified them in nine categories:

1. seas
2. seashores and estuaries
3. deserts
4. tundras

5. freshwater marshes
6. streams and rivers
7. lakes and ponds
8. grasslands
9. forests

Ecology and economy indicate that civilization will flourish best in conditions that approximate the most hospitable setting for humankind, which is the place where forest and grasslands meet. "Human civilization has so far reached its greatest development in what was originally forest and grasslands in temperate regions. . . . Man, in fact, tends to combine features of both grasslands and forests into a habitat for himself that might be called *forest edge*. . . . in grassland regions he plants trees around his homes, towns, and farms. . . . when man settles in the forest he replaces most of it with grasslands and croplands, but leaves patches of the original forest on farms and around residential areas. . . . man depends on grasslands for food, but likes to live and play in the shelter of the forest."[20] Every day, we experience the forest-edge habitat. It is a source of our ideas for buildings and landscapes.

What started pragmatically as an ecological habitat—the forests and grasslands, streams and rivers, lakes and ponds—has been transformed into the two great landscape design traditions of Western civilization.

They developed in the Italian and the French landscape gardens of the sixteenth and seventeenth centuries, and later in the English landscape gardens of the eighteenth and nineteenth centuries. Both garden design traditions use the same elements of nature—trees, plants, grasses, water—but in radically different compositions. They show different conceptions of the essence of nature; but they both are idealized expressions of the forest-edge habitat.

Landscape design uses the forest-edge habitat as a source because that natural environment provides for protection and production, shelter and openness, light and shade, structure and place. Building design has the same source. Architecture creates spatial conditions—arcades and colonnades, galleries and peristyles, loggias and porches, courtyards and cloisters—that resemble the clearings or edge of a forest.

In American architecture, nature's forest edge is a pervasive idea and image. It is embodied in spatial forms for both interiors and exteriors, for a wide range of building types, for both the public and the private realms, and for both vernacular buildings (constructions based on convention and traditions) and the designs of architects with widely divergent points of view.

American domestic architecture often has elements such as verandas and porches, for example, which are akin to the condition at the edge of a forest. The architect Calvert Vaux, Olmsted's partner in the design of Central Park, included many drawings of verandas and porches in his architectural stylebook. He said that "the *veranda* is perhaps the most specially American feature in a country house, and nothing can compensate for its absence."[21]

A vivid example of "nature" embodied in architecture is the United States Capitol building in Washington. It has entrance porches with colonnades, like a forest edge, leading into an interior colonnade surrounding a skylit domed hall, like a clearing in the forest. These ideas have a common source: the spatial forms of nature.

The Meanings of Nature

In Western civilization, the term "nature" has taken many meanings. Two ideas are persistent and recurring, despite their inherent opposition. Sometimes nature is taken as a model of regularity; sometimes it is revered for its irregularity. Each of these views is a basic metaphor, an idea displaying the essence of a system of values. In other words, each image embodies a distinct notion of culture, and of its major artifacts—buildings, landscapes, and cities. Emerson observed that the views of nature held by any people seem to "determine all their institutions."[22]

In both ancient and modern times, when nature was seen as regular in its growth, change, patterns, and forms, concepts were framed that expressed regularity. The geometry of nature was used as the basis of rational thought in every aspect of life, including aesthetics. A typical statement of this viewpoint might go something like this: "The work of every reasonable creature must derive its beauty from regularity, for reason is rule and order."[23]

The irregularity of nature has been greatly admired since the eighteenth century. The sense of irregular nature is expressed in the love of the wild, the picturesque, the rough and the rude, the passionate and the primitive, the romantic. Renoir, for example, said that artists should "proceed like nature, of whom they are always respectful pupils, [and] are on their guard never to transgress its fundamental law of irregularity."[24]

Just as the term "nature" has taken many meanings, so has the sense of "man in nature" changed, as a society and culture changed. One of the most evident physical manifestations of a culture is the design of a landscape garden—the conscious making of a space that is created to express man's ideal image of nature. It is in its own way a vision of "paradise." The word "paradise" originally meant "a walled garden." Although the garden is made of elements of nature, its form is determined by man's culture, by his ideas and values.

Different concepts of landscape gardens have come from different concepts of nature. Initially, in the Renaissance gardens of Italy and France, a geometric design was seen as natural, in the sense of an orderly, regular reality. The irregularity of the wilderness was not seen as orderly, and therefore was not the essence of nature. The geometric Renaissance garden was a deliberate abstraction, an idealization of nature. But, later, the emergence of the English landscape garden in the eighteenth century showed a dramatically different way of idealizing nature. Nature was then seen as curvilinear, not rectilinear; organic, not geometric.

Both the Italian-French garden tradition and the English garden tradition use the pastoral ideal as the basis of landscape form. The two traditions both seek to embody the "forest edge" in the landscape.

The Task of Architecture Is Function & Expression

To Protect

Could there be everyday life without architecture?

No, for two reasons.

First, as human animals, we must protect our bodies from hostile environments, so that we can live as individuals.

Second, as social animals, we must create protected places in our environment so that we can live together in groups.

> The first great consideration is that life goes on in an environment, but not merely in it, but because of it, through interaction with it.
>
> —JOHN DEWEY, ART AS EXPERIENCE[25]

What we build is a result of what we are. If our bodies were different, we would build different buildings, even different cities.

We have a big body that is upright, symmetrical side to side, and different front to back. We are bipedal; our legs can carry us forward, but not readily backwards or sideways. Our eyes look forward, with better long-distance than close-up vision. Our hands have grasping thumbs and fingers. We are a naked animal that no longer has protective covers for living in hot or cold environments. Our biological situation requires both clothing and buildings.

Our body is born without fur. We have warm bodies kept warm, from inside, but we become readily too cold or too hot—from outside. We build because our body needs thermal comfort. To be comfortable in a building, we must be able to do two things. We must control the ambient temperature of the air circulating around us, and we must control the radiant heat or cold that is beaming on us.

> *I really can't stay* / But, baby, it's cold outside
> *I've got to go 'way* / But, baby, it's cold outside
> *This evening has been* / Been hoping that you'd drop in
> *So very nice* / I'll hold your hands, they're just like ice

My mother will start to worry / Beautiful,
what's your hurry
And father will be pacing the floor / Listen to
the fireplace roar . . .
I really can't stay / Oh, baby, don't hold out
Ahh, but it's cold outside

—"BABY, IT'S COLD OUTSIDE"
(DUET BY FRANK LOESSER, 1944)

We build in different ways to control the
ambient and the radiant temperatures. For
ambient comfort, we enclose our buildings,
trap the air inside, heat or cool it, and
immerse our body in it. The window, an
opening in the wall, is the simplest device to
give us choices about our ambient temperature. Even the word, window, suggests its
Norse origin, *wind + eye*. Windows are not
only to look through, but sometimes to let in
breezes, for our comfort and pleasure.

For radiant comfort, because we lose heat from
our body directly to a frozen landscape outside,
or gain heat directly from the sun or a hot sidewalk, we protect windows with overhanging
eaves, movable shutters, shades, and curtains
that we can open or close for radiant *comfort*.
And, inside the house, we gather round a
fireplace hearth, for radiant *pleasure*.

Unlike other animals with thick skins that
serve as protecting shields, we have thin skins.

We build walls and roofs as our outer shields, to protect our bodies from threatening objects, like stones and bullets, as well as invaders, like burglars and bugs. We want our buildings to give us choices about what we let in and what we keep out. We build because our bodies need physical protection.

Architecture is the body's "third skin." We were born with a covering skin as standard equipment; later, as optional equipment, we choose clothing—hats, gloves, sweaters, and the like—to suit the climate and the occasion. Clothing creates the body's "second skin."

Clothing

Like architecture, clothing is simultaneously function and expression. Functionally, our clothing insulates us from the external environment. When we go outside, or come inside, we add or subtract layers of coats and sweaters. Conversely, to make ourselves comfortable in the heat, we wear thin fabrics—or very few clothes.

Clothing is intended to protect us from harm. We wear helmets when riding bicycles. We wear broad-brim hats to shade ourselves from the sun's rays. And sometimes, some of us wear bullet-proof vests.

If our clothes are intentionally functional, why are there such great differences in our "second skin"—even when the climate is the same, the place the same? The answer is obvious. Clothing expresses the occasion when it is being worn. It sends messages about the occasion, and about the person who is wearing it.

Some clothing is meant to be adaptable to many uses, akin to the loft buildings in nineteenth-century cast-iron industrial districts. Consider, for example, symbolic uniforms like the gray flannel suit and the little black dress, which can be worn on various occasions—especially in cities—and blue jeans, which are general purpose almost any time, almost anywhere.

Some clothing is intentionally "specialized"—designed to meet a specific set of performance requirements. Consider, for example, a surgeon going into a hospital operating room, putting on a gown as a protective layer. The green gown expresses the status of the wearer in the hospital culture. The design of the surgical gown is functional. But the color of the gown— green—is expressive. It sends the message that the wearer has scrubbed up to perform a highly skilled task.

Hat

At the top of the body, the hat is like architecture—it is simultaneously function and expression. As covering for the head, a hat is the "dome" of the body. In its many variations—as a cap, a fedora, a bowler, a straw hat, a helmet, a hard hat, a hood—the hat shelters the head from the outside, and creates a comfortable space inside (warm and snug, or cool and ventilated). It tells us about the occasion, the place, and the wearer . . . the red hat of the cardinal in a cathedral, the yellow hard hat of a construction worker on Broadway, the flamboyant helmet of a cyclist in the Tour de France, the scuba diver's helmet on a California beach. These hats are about "now," but sometimes, hats are about "then" . . . the veteran's cap on Memorial Day, the mortarboard at a college reunion, the Phillies World Series baseball cap. Hats evoke memories of past times, expressions of the present. Small wonder, then, that something that is out of style is seen as "old hat."

Considering the hat gives us many clues about why architecture matters. They are both about shelter, but there is a fundamental difference. A hat can be occupied by only one person at a time. Someone who tries to do two things simultaneously may be said to be "wearing two hats," but two people cannot be inside one hat. A hat is not a place of assembly.

Coat

Like a hat, a coat is both function and expression. It is like a portable tent, protecting the human body, performing for our well-being and comfort.

The coat gets its name from the medieval "coat of mail," a woven fabric of metal rings, strong enough to withstand slashing swords and penetrating knives as well as snakebites. The cloth "trench coat" came from the soldiers in the trenches of World War I; the thick wool "duffel coat" was the British navy's "convoy coat" in both world wars; the "greatcoat" was the luxurious cloth overcoat, with shoulder capes, worn by military officers and political leaders of imperial Europe: and the short, convenient, cloth "car coat" came from the twentieth-century suburban lifestyle. In each case, the coat had a meaning that came from its use. In that respect, a coat is profoundly like architecture.

While our physical environment sets performance requirements for a coat as a shelter, our society and culture set the stage for the coat to be expressive. A coat speaks about who we are and what we are doing. Its most useful devices—buttons and clasps, sleeves and collars, for example—are the parts most likely to be decorated with expressions of the wearer and the activity.

The coat and the building are similar in another respect. They often take the name of their materials—a fur coat, a cloth coat, a loden coat; a wooden house, a glass tower, a metal shed.

However, as a social form, the coat is fundamentally different from a building. A coat can shelter only one person at a time; a building can assemble many people and diverse activities. To live together in groups, to live in society, we build buildings, by necessity, and create architecture, by choice, to perform as our "third skin."

To Assemble

A building is our "third skin."

In our "second skin," clothing, we live as individuals. Clothing is not shared as a covering, with rare exceptions—say, a poncho at a football game. But when we want to assemble in groups, to live together in society, we need outer shelters, our "third skin."

We are social animals, and we need social shelters. Buildings do that job. They become architecture when, beyond serving to protect and shelter us, they become our shared, functional and expressive places. Architecture is an assemblage of places.

Space and Place

We all live in space. It is the space of nature, the continuous space we experience in everyday life, always with us and around us. It does not have edges and boundaries, or points and centers. Yes, it has its dark and light, its hot and cold, its up and down—but it is always boundless space. It is not particularized; it does not create a "sense of place." It is our general space.

We also live in local space. It is the space of architecture. It deals with the world here and now, and the world remembered. It is the domain of particular places.

> For it is still the case that no one lives in the world in general. Everybody, even the exiled, the drifting, the diasporic, or the perpetually moving, lives in some confined and limited stretch of it—"the world around here."
> —CLIFFORD GEERTZ, SENSES OF PLACE[26]

Personal Space

Personal space is the invisible "bubble" that surrounds our body. It is always with us. It influences everything that we do—and build—in our living environment, the size and shape of rooms, even the arrangement of furniture.

The size of our personal "bubble" is predictable; it varies with what we are doing, and with whom we are doing it. Psychologists have recognized that it is a kind of primary "territory."

Characteristically, our personal space is controlled by us, and respected—or invaded—by others. For example, when the New York Transit Authority needed to predict how many riders would fit into their new subway cars, it knew from experience that each standing person requires a "no-touch zone" in relationship to strangers (3.0 square feet of space). Although less than the area occupied by the open umbrella of someone walking along the sidewalk on a rainy day (5.0 square feet), it is more than the minimum comfortable space required when one is standing in a crowded elevator (1.5 square feet). The interior of a subway car or elevator is obviously an extreme case, but every architectural space is governed by the same considerations—how do we position ourselves in relationship to other people, to other objects, and to the enclosures that we create?

Shared Space

Architecture creates places that encourage people to be together—or others that discourage it.

Some places are centripetal. They draw people together and help them feel like staying. They engender social relationships. These are the social characteristics that we enjoy in a family living room, a dormitory lounge, a public plaza—when they are designed to form a social group.

On the other hand, some places are centrifugal. They separate people and discourage social interaction. They make it difficult for us to have pleasant contacts with others. These are the characteristics we often experience in subway stations and bus terminals; in airport corridors and waiting lounges; and, perhaps intentionally, in some fast-food restaurants.

Our social behavior in buildings is quite predictable, because architecture sets the stage for our actions. We often name rooms to indicate the actions for which we expect them to be the setting—for example, the dining room, the study, the bathroom, the lounge, the reading room, the meeting room. Sometimes, our actions take on the name of the place in which they regularly occur. We call people who work in the lobby of a legislature "lobbyists," and their activity is called "lobbying." And a "bank" (etymologically a "bench") is the place where we "bank" our money, transmitting it—originally, across a bench-like counter—to a "banker."

We position ourselves in space according to what we want to do, and some of our activities work best when they are highly structured in place and time. We create "a society of named places"[27] organized around fixed equipment—for example, an altar in a church, a bar in a restaurant, a reception desk in a hotel lobby, a fireplace hearth at home.

The kitchen and the bathroom contain fixed equipment at home. But most of our everyday actions use movable features—that is, chairs and sofas, desks and tables—which we can rearrange by choice. We arrange our chairs around a table for different functions, such as having a conversation (generally, sitting on two sides around the corner of the table), or working cooperatively (generally, next to each other on the same side of the table), or confronting each other (probably face-to-face across the table).

When people, furniture, and equipment are arranged in a room, more than the working functions are expressed. Host and guest, insider and outsider, status and role, hierarchy and power are made evident. Often, disputes arise over the shape of the table at a peace conference, because the shape is more than a functional issue.

For group interaction, the furniture and equipment of a room and the form of the space itself are at issue. For example, community meetings held in rooms with flat floors tend to be more interactive; meetings in rooms with sloping floors and speakers' platforms become inherently more structured.

Architecture is an enabling mechanism. It does not determine what we do, but it does make some things possible, and sometimes more probable. This is evident in how people actually behave in architectural places. For example, in two different forms of places—along a line, and around a center—social behavior is influenced in radically different ways.

Line and Center

Linear places encourage two kinds of group experiences. On linear routes—such as corridors in offices and dormitories, sidewalks on streets, even galleries in shopping malls—we walk past each other, see each other face-to-face, perhaps say hello, perhaps have a sense of a shared place.

Linear routes also enable us to walk side by side, alongside one another. Parades are great fun, and so is promenading along boulevards. Walking down the aisle of a church, or filing out of a school assembly hall, creates a sense of community because of the shared experience.

Centroidal places and linear routes are both social and architectural forms. They come from our nature—the human animal's systems of navigation. They have evolved into the functional and expressive frameworks of human habitats. Centroidal places are inherently suited for assembly, and linear routes are inherently suited for movement. We experience them from the small scale of the house to the large scale of the city, from room to region.

The contrast between centroidal and linear form is most evident in sacred spaces. Linear form embodies rituals of a procession to the altar. Centroidal form embodies the rituals that gather around the altar. The forms of these spaces are structured for different forms of ritual transactions.

Groups of people live in a "transactional" way, that is, in transactions with their structured-space environments.

Social and Physical

Architecture is double-rooted—it is simultaneously social and physical. Everything in architecture is experienced, and understood, both ways. Historically, for example, in medieval Europe, the word "church" originally meant the people, and later it also came to mean the building in which they assembled. The social form—and its name—came first, before the physical form, which took the same name.

> *Space is a society of named places.*
> —Claude Lévi-Strauss, *The Savage Mind*

To Embody

Architecture is the physical form of a social form. It embodies a social institution—a church, a school, a business corporation, a government, a family.

We live in many kinds of social institutions, and we know through experience that each has its own organization and its expected pattern of behavior. Its activities are structured in time as well as in space. At home, we speak of dinnertime in the dining room, and tell children that it is now bedtime in their bedrooms. We speak of occasions and places.

The close connection between a social institution and its physical place is evident in our language—the workplace, the courthouse, the clubhouse, the statehouse. Sometimes, a word means both an institution and a building—the church, the school, the shop. And in our imaginations, the thoughts and images are intertwined.

> [H]uman thought is basically both social and public. . . . its natural habitat is the house yard, the marketplace, and the town square.
> —CLIFFORD GEERTZ, *THE INTERPRETATION OF CULTURES*[28]

Ritual

Architecture is an institution's enabling mechanism, making it possible for people to perform its rituals. Whether the rituals are religious (in a sacred place) or secular (in a worldly place), architecture creates the action stage. It may be highly structured, as in a church or a criminal courtroom, where all aspects of the space and furnishings, the locations and movements of people, are determined by the rituals of the institution. Or it may be simply the sharing of a common place. For example, eating together in a shared place is one of the key rituals of social institutions as diverse as a family (in a kitchen or dining room), a college (in a student center), and a neighborhood (in a local bar or café).

A ritual such as entering a church, or a restaurant, may be a simple function, but its expression is a complex matter. The doorway sends signals about the role and status of the activity inside. We can "read" the institution by looking at its entry threshold—for example, the small glass door of a commercial office building; the wood-paneled door of a church; the columns and granite frame of a statehouse door; the canvas-canopied door of a restaurant. Indeed, one of the joys of architecture is its doorways, expressing what to expect inside—like an overture to a musical play.

Fixed Features

Architecture provides fixed features to serve as the settings for rituals. Consider, for example, an altar in a church—where should it be located? Should it be at the end of the church, as the focus of a perspectival space, or should it be in the center of the church, as the focus of a surrounding space? These two alternatives embody different ways of carrying out rituals, and sometimes different religious institutions.

A courtyard serves as a fixed feature for a vast range of institutions—colleges (the quadrangle), monasteries (the cloister), hotels (the atrium), and palaces (the royal court). A courtyard operates functionally as the center stage, and symbolically as the image of the institution itself.

The courtyard's corresponding urban form is the public square (such as Union Square in San Francisco) or a residential square in a neighborhood (such as Rittenhouse Square in Philadelphia). They are fixed features in the architecture of the city.

The house is, obviously, the architecture of the household. When fitted like a glove to its inhabitants, a typical single-family house has the most highly specialized collection of rooms in architecture. Each room and location in the house—living room, dining room, kitchen, bathroom, bedroom—conjures up its own role and image. Within household life, the interplay between privacy (in a room of one's own) and community (around the kitchen table, the fireplace, the TV set) generates the plan of the house. The social structure and the physical structure intertwine.

Political government is embodied in architecture. The castle, the palace, the capitol, the president's house, the statehouse, the house of parliament, the courthouse, the city hall—even the United Nations Headquarters—express their roles in governance. Some have evolved a typical form, so that their operations can be readily understood by the community. The United States Capitol building vividly expresses the two houses of Congress. It became the model for statehouses throughout the nation—especially because of its central dome, expressing the unity of the governed society.

In each of these places—church, house, statehouse, courtyard—architecture is an assemblage of people and their activities.

To Sustain

The built environment—buildings, landscapes, and cities—is like a palimpsest painting that does not start with a blank canvas. The building site exists before the building; and nature exists before it becomes a building site. We build in the palimpsest's here and now.

The built environment differs fundamentally from a work of art such as a painting hung on a wall or a sculpture sitting on a plaza. Once completed, a work of art does not need to continue to evolve and develop. It already "is." No one needs to add a beard to a portrait painting because society and fashion have changed.

The built environment is always "becoming." As society evolves, the built environment grows and changes, and architecture becomes engaged. By necessity, it participates when a social institution expands, or a street or neighborhood or district or an entire city changes; then, we ponder possibilities for improving and sustaining it.

Improving and sustaining work together, in different ways. Improving is a linear process, making something better within a defined scope; on the other hand, sustaining is a cyclical open-ended process, making things endure, renewed over and over.

Home Improvement

The built environment changes all the time, incrementally, because of home improvement and civic improvement.

Home improvement is more than an economic activity; it is a way of life. Popular culture has embraced it. A TV sitcom named *Home Improvement* first aired in 1991, and the documentary *This Old House* has been drawing a wide audience since 1979. Most homeowners report that they undertake repairs and improvement projects in their homes. Stores such as the Home Depot specialize in selling materials and tools for home improvement, and host classes to educate their customers.

Home improvement is about building here and now—incremental and local. Its cumulative impact on the built environment is huge.

Civic Improvement

Civic improvement calls upon architecture whenever change affects a city, a neighborhood, a street, a social institution. The shift may be caused by continuous technological, social, cultural, and economic changes, such as the rapid modernization of New York in the nineteenth century and that of Shanghai today. Or the changes may be caused by catastrophe, like the Great Fire of London in the seventeenth century, the Great Chicago Fire in the nineteenth century, or Hurricane Katrina and the earthquake and tsunami in Japan in recent times.

A new term, "civil architecture," should be used for the architecture required by a civil society. As in Napoleon's time, when civil engineering separated from the ancient practice of military engineering, we should now understand what civil architecture is, what it does, and how it fits.

Civil architecture works in the civic realm. It requires collaborative practice with engineering and the natural sciences, the humanities, and the social sciences. Its goal, civic improvement, has deep roots in American thought and practice, from Benjamin Franklin and the eighteenth-century Enlightenment, to John Dewey and twentieth-century pragmatism. Franklin proposed habits that would "secure private happiness and prosperity, together with a capacity for and devotion to civic improvement."[29]

Nowadays, civic improvement makes direct connections between design and public policy. Here is a statement from the city of Toronto website, which identifies three themes for civic improvement projects:

1. **Places**—"Places" is a Project Theme defined by opportunities to create outdoors "rooms" or distinctive "locations" in the public realm. . . .

2. **Routes**—"Routes" is a Project Theme that focuses on the opportunities for urban design improvements to the major elements of the City's street system. . . .
3. **Districts**—"Districts" is an integrated Project Theme comprised of interconnected and interrelated areas and neighbourhoods.[30]

To Perform

Performance is what makes architecture useful to us. Does the room enable you to see and hear what's happening? Does the entrance guide you in, and then do you know where to go? Do the walls keep out the wind and rain? Can we live there? In all these ways architecture has instrumental value.

Building performance differs from culture to culture. How to protect the human body, how to provide comfort, how to offer privacy: these choices differ between cultures. The historical Japanese house had a flexible separation of inside and outside environments, consisting of lightweight sliding panels, translucent white paper in thin frames. In contrast, the historical Western house had solid enclosing walls—stone, brick, wood, metal—with recognizable windows and doors serving as filters between the inside and outside.

Outcomes

Because a building is an enabling mechanism for our living—as individuals, or groups, or societies. It enables us to protect ourselves, to live together in groups, to house our social institutions. This outcome is the "possibility" argument for architecture's having instrumental value.

On the other hand, a building makes it probable that we will be comfortable—that is, warm or cool, safe and secure. It makes it likely that we will see and meet others, and that we will find our way out in case of a fire. Having a probable outcome is the argument supporting architecture's performance value.

If the "probabilist" argument were carried to an extreme, architecture would become a kind of environmental determinism. Then, a building could determine what we can do, and how we can do it. Obviously, some buildings, such as maximum security prisons, need to be highly probabalist in their performance. But, fortunately, most of life—and most architecture—is more concerned with possibilities than with absolute performance. We want to have choice.

Choices

Choice is the essence of design. When we design something—a room, a doorway, or a building—we are making choices. We consider costs and benefits, and we deal with our likes and dislikes. These choices require balancing acts; they express what a social scientist or political philosopher would call our "weighted preferences." Choice is the essence of economics and politics—and of design.

Various realms of philosophy influence us when we are designing—aesthetics is concerned with beauty and pleasure; epistemology is concerned with knowledge; logic is concerned with order and structure; and moral philosophy—ethics—deals with right or wrong in our actions.

Questions of good and bad, right and wrong, are at the heart of architecture as a political act. Can we have school buildings that foster learning; hospitals that support health care; and neighborhoods that nurture a sense of community? To enable, to support, to foster—these are architectural performance requirements. Architecture is an enabling mechanism.

To Express

Architecture is expressive. It goes beyond serving functional needs of individuals and groups and institutions. It expresses (it shows, conveys, exhibits, represents, indicates, communicates) facts and feelings, places and occasions, realities and ideals.

Facts

Architecture can express facts about itself, such as the structural system that keeps it standing, dealing with the vertical forces of gravity, and withstanding the horizontal forces of winds. Actual structures—such as skeleton frameworks made of columns and beams, or vaulted structures made of ribs and arches—can be vividly expressed. In Romanesque and Gothic architecture, the expression of the vaulted stone structure— and its space and light—create "the house of God."

On the other hand, a building is not required to express facts about itself. It can keep some facts hidden, unexpressed. It is a matter of choice in the creation of the architectural form. For example, the building can display an image of the actual structure, not the authentic structure itself. In Italian Renaissance and English Georgian buildings, representations of Classical columns and beams were applied to the walls; they were not the actual structure of the building, but the expression of an idealized structure.

Architecture not only embodies a social institution; it expresses facts about it. What is the building? Is it a house, a college, or a factory? How it is organized? How does it work? Moreover, a building can do more than express the function of its social institution; it can express its spirit—the orderliness of law courts, the sacredness of houses of worship, the friendliness of resort hotels, the joys of movie theaters. We read buildings, not only for facts, but for expressions of human feelings.

Feelings

Architecture is like art, according to the philosopher Suzanne Langer,[31] when it creates forms that are expressions of human feelings.

Musical expression goes beyond the notes. Music can express a range of emotions; often a composer will specify an expression mark (a sign or word indicating the expression required of a performer) to be part of the musical score, as a guide to the performer.

In the theater, playwrights often specify the feelings to be expressed by the actors. One author can ask for "a quiet level voice without expression of any sort." Another can specify that "an expression of anger spread across his face." The expression can be specified by the writer, going beyond the words of the play, as a guide to the actor.

Architecture's users are akin to music's performers and the theater's actors. Sometimes, their functional performance is signaled by a legally required written or graphic message that specifies an action, like a "Fire Exit" sign. But everyday functional performance—actions like "enter" and "gather"—is guided by the design of architectural space. The expression of function is at the beginning of architecture. Whereas in music expression goes beyond the notes, in architecture emotional expression goes beyond the function.

Emotional expression in architecture relies on symbolic messages embedded in the architecture—its space and structure; its colors, textures, and materials; and its organization of experience. Unlike musical composition with its expression marks, architectural composition does not need to add literal signs on the wall to specify an emotional performance. We need not install placards saying, "Feel friendly" or "Be harmonious." The expressive signs can be inherent in the design.

Because they come from our experiences in everyday living, architectural expressions vary wonderfully. That is why we enjoy walking around cities, looking at buildings, understanding them functionally, and experiencing them emotionally. They can be emotionally

> comforting or threatening,
> civil or brutal,
> delicate or crude,
> noble or frivolous,
> harmonious or discordant,
> depressing or exciting,
> calm or shocking.

Materials and Constructions

Expression in architecture comes from its construction. Building materials are naturally expressive. For example, we experience a brick-and-stone wall as emotionally "warm" compared to a steel-and-glass wall. With good reason. Brick and stone are actually warmer to touch because they are poor conductors of heat. They take away heat from our hand at a slower rate than do metal and glass; therefore, we experience them as relatively warm. Function and expression are deeply connected in our experience.

Other Places and Other Times

When we look at a building—any building, no matter how simple or complex—we also see it as something other than what it actually is. We might say, "That looks like Oxford," when actually it is a town in New Jersey. Or we might say, "That looks like a forest," when it is actually the interior of a church. We seek to associate what we are viewing with other things—other times and places, other people and institutions, even with nature itself. We enjoy making the association in our imagination. It helps us cope with what we are experiencing. It enriches our understanding.

Sometimes, a deliberate reference to another time is important to a social institution, whose architecture is used to make the association. For example, "collegiate Gothic" was the architectural language of some American universities seeking to be associated—at least in our imagination—with the medieval origins of the Oxford and Cambridge colleges.

Referring to a different time, some American colleges and universities sought to associate themselves with the eras of ancient Greece and Rome. The Classical style of architecture was intentionally used, to create an association with the "classics" in the arts and humanities.

In his design for the new University of Virginia campus (plate 4), Thomas Jefferson relied on the Classical language of architecture. For the university—and, indeed, in his proposals for all public institutions—he advocated ancient Roman architecture as the appropriate expression of the new American democracy, a direct reference to the democracy of classical times.

Human Body

Sometimes, a building refers to something we know and experience all the time—our body.

To construct space that we can understand, we take the human body as a model of order and measurement. We see this model not as a pure abstraction, nor as a literal representation of our bodies. Rather, it is a source of what the mathematician Henri Poincaré called an "instinctive geometry." It is our understanding of how we are structured—composed of recognizable parts; organized around a vertical axis; sometimes symmetrical from side to side, but not symmetrical from top to bottom; and having a front and a back—like architecture.

Social Institutions

Social institutions express their status, role, and power in architectural forms. Especially interesting are the dome and the tower.

The dome is our most monumental form, ever since the ancient Pantheon in Rome. In the contemporary world our most powerful institutions are sometimes expressed by the same form: the dome of St. Paul's, the Church of England cathedral in London, is religious; its architectural counterpart in Washington, the dome of the United States Capitol building in Washington, is secular.

Like a dome, a tower can be either secular or religious. In early Manhattan, two of the most vivid expressions of the emerging metropolis were the religious tower of Trinity Church and the secular tower of the Woolworth Building.

Towers compete with domes as political expressions—the Houses of Parliament in

London, the City Hall tower in Philadelphia, Huey Long's State Capitol in Louisiana. And towers express corporate power and character, sometimes with excellent architecture like Colonel McCormick's Tribune Tower in Chicago.

Architecture is an investment of the institution's current resources and an instrument for its future development. When a university or a corporation plans a new research laboratory, the decision indicates its strategic plan for the future. Similarly, the building of affordable housing and community facilities is an indicator of the priorities of a society. As a use of resources, architecture—the embodiment of institutions—expresses their economic and social values. To learn about social institutions, read their buildings.

An Ideal

Sometimes, architecture expresses an ideal—an ideal natural landscape like a mountain; or an ideal institution in a golden age; or an ideal cosmos; or an ideal geometry.

If the dome is an architectural image of the dome of heaven and the vertical tower marks the axis of the earth, they both express the ideal order of the cosmos. On the other hand, the ideal society of a golden age is quite different—it is a matter of our choice and interpretation. We have some town halls that are intentionally Gothic because of our concept of an idealized medieval community, and other town halls that are Classical because of our concept of the Greek and Roman roots of an idealized democracy.

Architecture sometimes looks toward a future golden age. In the development of modernism, optimistic architects such as Louis Sullivan (1856–1924) sought the architecture of a democracy, and Walter Gropius (1883–1969) sought the architecture of a modern industrial society.

The Legacy of Architecture Is Form

Experiencing Form

Architecture is not autonomous. We actually experience it in a setting, some-where, some-place.

As we approach a building, we experience **architecture as mass**. We see it as a body. We see its outline and silhouette; we observe its solids and voids. We see its composition, its overall shape and its parts, as if we were looking at a sculpture.

As we stand near a building, we experience **architecture as surface**. We see it as a fabric, colored, dark or light, textured smooth or rough, transparent or opaque. We see it as a graphic composition, as if we were looking at a drawing or a painting.

When we go inside a building, we experience **architecture as space**. A building is like a bottle; we experience space as if we were inside the bottle. The inside space has shape; architecture structures the space. It creates a sense of place.

As we move through space, we experience **architecture as movement**. We inhabit a series of "named places," in sequence. We walk from place to place, up and down, on floors and stairs, in movement through time.

Structural Form

Form may be understood to be a shape, but the shape is only an *external* aspect—an outer boundary. For example, while a lake has a shape, it has no structure. When a shape also has an *internal* structure, an inner organization, then it has *form*.

Architecture as "structure" has two meanings: one involves the materials and methods in its construction; the other involves the arrangement of parts in its organization.

Today, the notion of architecture as structure applies to many things other than buildings. For example, when the *Financial Times* newspaper reports that the architecture of a company is being rebuilt from within, it refers not to the physical-structure sense of architecture, the buildings of the company, but to the organizational-structure sense of architecture—that is, the company's departments and divisions, products and services.

The physical structure and the organizational structure can create an "inclusive" sense of architecture, as was set forth by Vitruvius as "Fundamental Principles of Architecture" in *De Architectura* (On Architecture), first century BCE, book 1, chapter 2.

> *Architecture depends on:*
>
> *Order,*
> *Arrangement,*
> *Eurythmy,*
> *Symmetry,*
> *Propriety,*
> *Economy.*

In architecture, the test of structural form is performance—does it work? For example, does the **structure as construction** securely hold up the walls and roof, and does the **structure as organization** effectively relate people and tasks?

Sometimes, architecture intentionally creates a "tight fit" between its two meanings, physical structure and organizational structure. For example, the typical Gothic cathedral had a linear plan and vaulted spaces—the nave, aisles, transept, and apse—that embodied its processional liturgy. Similarly, a typical Frank Lloyd Wright Usonian house (plate 5) had an articulated private bedroom wing in contrast to a free-flowing living/dining/kitchen/hearth that embodied open family life.

Sometimes, architecture intentionally creates a "loose fit" rather than a tight one, to enable changes in the future. For example, a typical loft building of early industrial districts located its fixed features, elevators and stairs, along a side wall to provide an open loft. Similarly, a contemporary art museum like the Centre Pompidou in Paris, in contrast to the old articulated set of "cabinet galleries," now has large modules of open space, ready to be subdivided according to the occasion.

Social Form

Home, state, church, school, market, and workplace are social institutions. They are organized in expected patterns of behavior, in structured places. They are social forms, and they are also physical forms.

The family is at home in a place called "home"; the social institution of religion is embodied in a church; the social institution of education is embodied in a school; the government is embodied in halls of government.

Politics is one of the most expressive activities in society, and political power, as we've seen, is embodied in architectural form: the town hall, the statehouse, the English Houses of Parliament, the French Chamber of Deputies, the dome of the United States Capitol building. The functional organization of our national legislature is expressed by two "houses" (the Senate and the House of Representatives) in Classical temples, flanking a central dome. By contrast, the state of Nebraska has a different form of legislature—a single chamber—in a capitol building with a single tower.

The task of architecture is to make function and expression fit together.

Transparency

In our times, transparency is almost always seen as a good idea.

We want our governments to be open, democratic, and transparent; we want our businesses to be fair, honest, and transparent;

we want our public institutions to be understandable, responsive, and transparent.

Small wonder, then, that we try to express transparency in our architecture. For example, the architects invited to participate in the design competition for the new American Embassy in London were informed by the State Department that their "expressive challenge is to give form to the core beliefs of our democracy—transparency, openness, and equality."[32]

And when the Los Angeles Police Department was "handed the keys to its new headquarters. . . . [Chief of Police] Bratton said the glass facade of the 500,000-square-foot structure represents the new LAPD of the 21st century, an era of transparency for a department once resistant to public scrutiny."[33] Here, the chief was trying to make a direct connection between the building's glass and the department's organizational transparency. Alas, in daylight, the building is quite opaque; the glass facade acts like a mirror, reflective rather than transparent. Caveat emptor: let the buyer—the citizen—beware.

By contrast, the utopian ideal of transparency was truly achieved in the design and fabrication of the Apple Store on Fifth

Avenue, New York (plate 2). The entire structure is clear glass. The patent claim submitted by Steve Jobs et al. (United States Design Patent US D478,999S, August 26, 2003) said, modestly, "The staircase has a transparent character."

Often, transparency is even more a social requirement than a visual one. For example, at the Institute for Advanced Study in Princeton—admittedly not a populist institution—the director sought to increase awareness of the overall makeup of the institute and to encourage casual interaction among its members. He asked the architects of its new dining hall to include "social transparency" as a planning requirement. The design responded; for almost fifty years now, it has been providing "social transparency" in the layout of destinations, walkways, balconies, and stairways (enabling its members to see others coming and going, from the several parts of the institute), even the arrangement of tables in the dining hall; and it offers "physical transparency" in the cubistic layers of glass and screens, the interpenetration of inside halls and outside gardens.

In architecture, transparency is both physical and social. Its physical transparency comes from our *looking at the physical appearance*, and its social transparency comes from our *reading the social organization*. Looking and reading, using the eye and the mind, experiencing architecture.

Parts and Assemblies: Modularity

Ever since classical antiquity, some sort of "modularity" has been used by architects and builders to make things fit together. Initially, the "modules" were units of measurement that served as guidelines for the proportions of a building and its parts, such as columns and frames, doors and windows, vaults and domes. Modules determined the size of all parts of an "order." According to the historian John Summerson,[34] the aim was to achieve a harmony of parts. To make things fit, the Classical architect's task was "combinatorial."

Modularity is also a modern idea, embodied in the "organic" architecture of Frank Lloyd Wright, the industrial design products of the Bauhaus, the "modulor" grid of Le Corbusier, the constructivism of the Centre Pompidou in Paris, and the modular urbanism of Rockefeller Center in New York. To make things fit together, the modern architect's task remains combinatorial.

Not only in architecture, but also in art and science, fit combinations have been based on some sort of modularity. For example, in a sixteenth-century *scientific* treatise on applied geometry titled *The Art of Measurement*, the *artist* Albrecht Dürer designed a new Gothic typeface based on square modules.[35] Similarly, modern painters and sculptors have created "modular" art works, such as Piet Mondrian's abstract painting *Broadway Boogie-Woogie* (1942–1943) and Tony Smith's geometric steel sculpture *Moses* (1968). Even in the seemingly spontaneous, improvisational sculptures of John Chamberlain, the idea of fit is embodied in "the natural, innate interconnection between sections of his sculptures."[36] Similarly, in science, modern ecologists claim that modularity is necessary for "understanding the development and evolution of natural complex systems."[37] In 1917, the biologist D'Arcy Thompson published a seminal book, *On Growth and Form*,[38] analyzing the order of natural and man-made structures.

Parts and Assemblies: Articulations

In architecture, combinations are "articulated"—they are expressed on surfaces, and in spaces. Historian E. H. Gombrich suggested two reasons for articulations, which he named "structural" and "explanatory."[39]

Structural articulation expresses the organized **existence** of something. For example, the construction materials and methods may be clearly articulated—the ribs and vaults of Gothic architecture, the frames and panels of modern architecture. On the other hand, the construction may be only alluded to—for example, flat expressions of columns and beams on the walls of Renaissance architecture. Or it may not be revealed at all—"look Ma, no hands!"—creating shock and awe. When taken to extremes, the opposite of structural articulation is **chaos**.

Explanatory articulation expresses the **purpose** of something. For example, porticoes of Classical architecture, vaulted porches of medieval architecture, transparent lobbies of modern architecture are articulated as ways to enter a building. Whether on a city street (plate 6) or in an open landscape, the experience of architecture requires explanatory articulations that are recognizable, understood, and shared. The opposite, where "the elements of an object and its outlines are obscured by conflicting information,"[40] is confusion and **camouflage**.

Chaos and camouflage have a common characteristic: they both lack a "sense of order." That may sound ominous, but, according to Gombrich, "we must ultimately be able to account for the most basic fact of aesthetic experience, the fact that delight lies somewhere between boredom and confusion."[41]

Parts and Assemblies: Scale

Experiencing "scale" is a delight that lies somewhere between boredom and confusion. When everything has exactly the same scale, life seems mechanically inhuman; but it may also seem inhuman when everything is chaotically unrelated in scale.

Before the Industrial Revolution, the scale of buildings and cities was limited by the human body. How far one could routinely walk in any given direction and return was limited in the horizontal dimension; and how far one could readily climb stairs was limited in the vertical dimension.

Two industrial inventions of the "first machine age" changed everything—Mr. Otis's safety elevator and Mr. Ford's Model T car. Frank Lloyd Wright predicted that if Americans were forced to choose between the elevator and the automobile, they would choose the automobile. So far, he has been right—growth and form created a new horizontal scale.

Meanwhile, Mr. Otis's elevator created a new vertical scale. Tall structures had been regularly built, of course, for religious, civic, and symbolic purposes, but not for conventional everyday living. At the end of the nineteenth century, in Lower Manhattan, the tallest structure was the tower of Trinity Church; the tallest tower in the world for a short period of time was City Hall in Philadelphia. A paradigm shift occurred during the rebuilding of Chicago's Loop business district, where the solid brick Monadnock Building was the world's tallest load-bearing masonry building, while, nearby, the steel frame of the Reliance Building and its modular "Chicago window" heralded a new scale of urban structures.

For a while, it seemed that the design of a tall building should be like a Classical "column," having three parts: a bottom, a middle, and a top. It became the civilized model for Louis Sullivan's urban buildings. But his disciple Frank Lloyd Wright explored other possibilities, such as a crystalline group of residential towers for St. Mark's-in-the-Bouwerie (New York, 1928), and a mile-high spike, "The Illinois" (Chicago, 1956), that foreshadowed a new scale to come.

Size and scale are related—but they are not the same. Size is an *actual* dimension; scale is a *relative* matter.

> Grand scale
> **Human scale**
> Diminutive scale

We experience human scale all the time. It connects everything to the experience of our body—for example, climbing the risers and treads of a staircase, walking through a swinging door, looking out a bay window, sitting on a front porch. Human scale is the basic measure of architecture, the source of its proportions and rhythms.

But there is more than human scale involved in the experience of architecture. We intentionally build at a larger scale for some places and occasions, and at a smaller scale for others. Along a city street with similar-size buildings, for example, we might walk past a bank with a monumental-scale entryway next to a jewelry shop with intimate-scale windows, a public library with a grand-scale porch next to a coffee shop with diminutive sidewalk seating. Look at places like Disneyland and Princeton's Palmer Square that are intentionally designed at a smaller-than-human scale; or the Federal Triangle between the Capitol and the White House in Washington, DC, intentionally designed at a grand scale; as well as vernacular places like Seattle's Pike Place (plate 8A) and Hoboken's Washington Street that delight us because of their diversity of scale.

Scale is about the fit of something, in its setting—a staircase in a building, an entrance on a street, a tower block in a city. Should they blend in, or stand out?

"Fit" is always the question.

In London, after the Great Fire of 1666, Christopher Wren proposed regulations for rebuilding the district with "blend-in" vernacular street walls, and "stand-out" strategic places for church steeples.

In nineteenth-century Paris, the architectural design of the Opera House at the head of its own boulevard was a grand "blend in," whereas the twentieth-century design of the Opera House in Sydney Harbour was a glorious "stand out." In different ways, they both "fit."

Along Fifth Avenue in New York, the twin spires of St. Patrick's Cathedral "stand out," but directly across the street, Rockefeller Center's group of four low buildings "blend in," while its tallest tower is set back and dramatically "stands out" (plate 7).

How to fit is the essence of design.

Delight and Beauty

Architecture's ancient triad, "firmitas, utilitas, venustas," favored by Roman architect-engineer Vitruvius, became "firmness, commodity and delight" in a seventeenth-century English translation by author Sir Henry Wotton. "Venustas," the Latin word for "beauty," was translated as "delight."

However, beauty and delight are fundamentally different. When we experience architecture, beauty is something **it** may have, whereas delight is something **we** may have.

Style

From time to time, we imagine the world differently. We invent new forms for things, new "styles." Historians claim that the concept of style is necessary for the understanding of history, because it expresses what we are thinking, doing, and making, in everyday life.

We can recognize style in many ways:

According to its place of origin French style

Japanese style

According to its architect	Palladian style
	Frank Lloyd Wright style
According to its materials	Shingle style
	Cast-iron style
According to its design school	Beaux-Arts style
	Bauhaus style
According to its aesthetic	Classical style
	Romantic style
According to its politics	Conservative style
	Progressive style
According to its character	Vernacular style
	Industrial style
According to its time of origin	Medieval style
	Modern style

Modern Architecture

Ex nihilo nihil fit.
Nothing can be made or emerge out of nothing.
Nothing in the world can arise without a cause.
—PARMENIDES, SIXTH CENTURY BCE

"Modern" architecture has emerged many times.

First, it was born in the Renaissance in Italy, when "modern" history was separated from "ancient" and "medieval" history, and new architecture was based on the philosophy of humanism, classicism, and geometrical perspective.

Second, it was born in the industrial age in England, when the Agricultural Revolution and the Industrial Revolution changed the modes of production, distribution, and consumption in society.

Third, it was born in the aesthetic revolution in Europe and America, during the late nineteenth and early twentieth centuries, expressing the constructive visions of cubism and constructivism, abstraction and expressionism.

Fourth, it was born again, during the late twentieth century's new digital age, using computational design technologies and non-Euclidian geometries, expressing new constructive visions of surface, mass, space, and movement.

The modern style is linked to: the politics of social democracy; industrial methods of building; abstract art, cubism, and constructivism; the Bauhaus and the International Style; in brief, functionalism.

Functionalism has been a recurring style since classical times. Its clearest statement, "Form follows function," was derived from nineteenth-century biological science and industrial technology. The idea was best expressed by the question "Does it work?"

> *Beauty as the promise of Function . . .*
> *Action as the presence of Function . . .*
> *Character as the record of Function.*
> —HORATIO GREENOUGH, SCULPTOR
> (1805–1852)[42]

The new modern style is linked to: the politics of individualism; economic and cultural globalization; post-structuralism and deconstructivism; computational methods of design and production; in brief, expressionism.

The crucial difference is that **the modern** wanted to build shared, reproducible environments. A favorite book was architect Percival and poet Paul Goodman's *Communitas*. As the style-to-end-all-styles, it wanted to become the norm. It wanted to build social and physical places that fit together, in intentional groupings. For **the modern**, the keyword was **community**.

The new modern wants to build unique environments, to become a "spectacle." Shock is the new norm. It is intentionally unstable:

"walls that cant and lean, roofs that bubble and heave, buildings that look as if they are instantly ready to take off into space or collapse."[43] A favorite book is Ayn Rand's novel *The Fountainhead*. For **the new modern** the keyword is **iconic**.

An **other-modern** is always emerging, somewhere, from the problems as well as the possibilities of **the modern**. For example, modernist Louis Kahn explored the making and meaning of "the room," challenging the continuous, flowing space of fellow modernist Le Corbusier's "free plan." (One published interview with Kahn was titled, "How'm I Doing, Corbusier?") At the same time that Kahn was working inside architecture (on the design of a laboratory at the University of Pennsylvania), he also was working outside (on the social and physical form of Center City Philadelphia). Such a progressive **other-modern** is needed again, to invent architecture inside and outside.

Civic Form

> *By its form, as by the manner of its birth,*
> *the city has elements at once of biological*
> *procreation, organic evolution, and*
> *aesthetic creation. It is both natural object*
> *and a thing to be cultivated; . . . something*

> lived and something dreamed; it is the
> human invention, par excellence.
> —CLAUDE LÉVI-STRAUSS[44]

For the growth and form of cities, civic populism and civic monumentalism are seemingly contrary styles, but we need both. We cannot live together in cities without them.

Civic monumentalism is the city's long-lasting structure: its services and transportation infrastructures; its boulevards and avenues; its squares and plazas; its buildings and landmarks.

Civic populism is the city's fabric for everyday living, working, shopping: its streets and sidewalks; its local centers and neighborhoods; its particular places.

Both styles of civic form, populism and monumentalism, can be seen in images from the past. For example, a large wall fresco in Siena displays civic populism (plate 1A), and a painted wood panel in Urbino displays civic monumentalism (plate 1B).

The Siena fresco painted ca. 1337–1339 by Ambrogio Lorenzetti was commissioned by the Nine, the chief magistrates of Siena, for their large chamber in the new Palazzo Pubblico. It displays the impact of "Good

Government" (in contrast to its twin fresco across the chamber, "Bad Government") in a detailed panorama of the city and countryside—people and their animals streaming through the gate in the city wall, tightly packed, irregularly spaced diverse buildings, tradesmen working in open shops, a circle of nine young dancers in the street. The overall form of the city comes from its civic infrastructure (essentially, the walls and gates, streets and marketplaces, wells and fountains) containing an irregular assembly of thick-walled structures, with narrow vertical windows above open-arched arcades. Architectural expressions of power, whether political or religious, are not dominant—the Palazzo Pubblico and the piazza are absent, and the cathedral's dome and tower are barely seen on the skyline. Instead, there are vignettes of economic and social activities, the spontaneity of everyday street life, the *vita activa*. The painting, commissioned and displayed by the government itself, actually glorifies civic populism.

The Urbino panel, known as *The Ideal City*, was painted ca. 1480, possibly by Piero della Francesca, over a carefully constructed perspective drawing attributed, after recent X-ray and reflectograph study, to the architect-philosopher Leon Battista Alberti. The exact date and purpose of the painting are uncertain. The composition is like a monumental stage set, in bright white light, just before the action begins. There are no people to be seen, perhaps indicating the belief that an ideal society will be produced by an ideal place. The architecture uses a Classical vocabulary— walls with columns and pilasters, framed windows and doors, open arcades and loggias. Calm and harmonious, clean and hygienic, it even has two symmetrical wells from which the people may draw their water—obviously an orderly society. The painting embodies Renaissance ideals of mathematics, perspective, and form—a geometric grouping of buildings, similar in scale and rhythm, forming the sides of a monumental plaza, with a rotunda at its center point. The painting glorifies civic monumentalism.

Civic Monumentalism

In America, civic monumentalism arrived with the first settlers and was embodied in ideal plans for new cities. In contrast to the medieval street patterns of Boston and Lower Manhattan, two of our earliest settlements— New Haven, Connecticut, and Philadelphia, Pennsylvania—were built according to civic designs that were rectangular, symmetrical, and monumental.

New Haven was the first planned city in the colonies. Laid out in 1638 by the settlers' surveyor, its geometric grid of streets formed nine equal squares, like a checkerboard. It had ancient parentage: the plans of Roman military camps, and the theories of the Roman engineer Vitruvius—for example, in the orientation of the street grid to catch breezes and avoid diseases. Many Renaissance plans used a common vocabulary—a grid of straight streets and paved plazas—but New Haven was different, because its central square was an open lawn under a canopy of trees. "The Green," as it was named, has remained New Haven's central place. Yale College's "Old Campus" is next to the Green. The town hall, post office, businesses, and banks face the Green. In the nineteenth century, three monumental churches were built on the Green; in a "civic oration" by Rev. Dr. Leonard Bacon, the Green was praised "not as a park or mere pleasure ground, but as a place for public buildings, for military parades and exercises, for the meeting of buyers and sellers, for the concourse of the people, for all such public uses as were reserved of old by the Forum at Rome and the 'Agora' (called in our English bibles 'the market') at Athens."[45] New Haven's grid plan and center square became the model for America's civic monumentalism.

William Penn's 1683 plan of Philadelphia envisioned a new settlement larger than London or Paris at the time. Extending two miles between the Delaware and Schuylkill Rivers, in a wooded wilderness named "Pennsylvania," Penn's ideal "green country town" had a geometric form, a rectangular grid of streets, a civic square at the crossing of its two major axes, and a residential square in each of its four quadrants. The plan was also a regional concept—the purchase of a homesite in town was paired with a property in the surrounding countryside. At the end of the nineteenth century, in Philadelphia's industrial age, a new City Hall was built on the central square—it was the world's tallest habitable structure, topped by an illuminated clock tower and a bronze statue of William Penn. During the early twentieth century, a wide diagonal was cut through the original street grid, like a French tree-lined boulevard, connecting the City Hall to a grand new landmark, the Philadelphia Museum of Art, at the gateway to a regional green park. Philadelphia embodied civic monumentalism in architecture, civic design, and regional form.

America built a rectangular country. Thomas Jefferson in 1785 wrote the first congressional legislation calling for a "rectangular land survey." From the outset, the survey was geometric in form, but simultaneously philosophical, political, economic, and social in content. (Decades later, Jefferson worked with similar intentions when he designed the "Academical Village" for a university [plate 4].) The new survey system replaced the ancient "metes and bounds" method, in which a place was identified according to its physical features, such as rocks, trees, streams, or other unique markers; by contrast, in the new rectangular survey system, a place was identified according to its position in a matrix, a rectangular grid. The consequences were profound. For the new nation, the grid structured the territories; for its political functions, it set governmental boundaries and identified townships, counties, and states; and for its civic designs, it created the groundwork, the land structure, the civic "field."

America has used the rectangular grid in two ways—as an expression of ideal order, and as a practical mechanism to fit things together. At its best, the grid creates "group form," a civic framework for buildings and landscapes, such as the street grid of Manhattan laid out by the commissioners of New York in 1811, and the "Group Plan" for its civic center laid out by the city of Cleveland in 1903. The grid has nurtured great civic streets—Fifth Avenue in New York, Commonwealth Avenue in Boston, Wilshire Boulevard in Los Angeles; and the grid has also harbored great civic places— twenty-two leafy squares in Savannah, Rockefeller Center in New York (plate 7),

Pioneer Square in Portland, Union Square in San Francisco. Over the centuries, the grid's theory and practice have evolved, for new sources of power, new types of vehicles, new types of roadways and transitways, creating new streetscapes for new societies.

America began to celebrate itself at the end of the nineteenth century. Chicago was the fulcrum. Its World's Columbian Exposition (1893) commemorated Columbus's voyage from the Old World to the New World; it also celebrated the New America. Chicago looked backward and forward. On the one hand, its exposition's designers—a collaborative group of architects, landscape architects, painters, and sculptors unequaled in American history—used the imagery of the European past to propose a fantasy for the future: the "White City." On the other hand, the actual Chicago was rebuilding itself, following the Great Fire of 1871, in the new style of the industrial age—structures with metal skeletons, the "Chicago frame," and rectangular facades with large panels of glass, the "Chicago window."

Chicago evoked civic pride. In 1909, the powerful businessmen of the Commercial Club sponsored preparation of the comprehensive "Plan of Chicago," now known as the "Burnham Plan" in honor of its chief architect, Daniel H. Burnham. The Plan of Chicago was essentially a framework for civic improvements—the lakefront (plate 8B), streets and boulevards, railroads and terminals, regional highways, waterways and harbors, parks and natural landscapes. It was one of the great civic documents in American history.

The politics of the Progressive Era, the architecture of the White City, and the civic monumentalism of the Plan of Chicago were embodied in the City Beautiful movement (plate 6). It had aristocratic roots in Europe, especially in the cities and landscapes of France; but, in America, it addressed local problems—sanitation, housing, overcrowded neighborhoods, and political corruption. It was a reform movement. Its goal was civic improvement. The phrase "City Beautiful" is somewhat misleading today, implying a superficial aesthetic for civic design; however, as the muckraking journalist Henry Demarest Lloyd wrote about the White City, it revealed "possibilities of social beauty, utility, and harmony of which they had not been able even to dream"[46] (plate 8B).

The City Beautiful movement became a style in civic design. Although the concept of "style" is widespread in the arts and architecture, it remains a rarity in the history of civic design. It was a popular choice at the time, combining the public arts of architecture, landscape design, and city planning, and the fine arts of painting and sculpture.

The elegant geometry of New York City's Bryant Park, sitting behind the new Public Library building on Fifth Avenue (plate 6), was originally designed in the City Beautiful landscape style, but it was later transformed because of the work of Jane Jacobs's colleague William "Holly" Whyte. Whyte spent most of his life observing "the social life of small urban spaces,"[47] and Bryant Park was rebuilt according to his ideas. It now hosts a swirling mix of people, movable tables and chairs, and, often, an after-dark jazz or film festival. As Bryant Park shows, civic populism can happily fit within civic monumentalism.

Civic Populism

Twentieth-century America received two brilliant proposals for the future of its cities, one by Daniel Burnham in 1909, another by Jane Jacobs in 1961. They could hardly have been more different. One demonstrated civic monumentalism; the other explored civic populism.

Daniel Burnham worked as an architect, Jane Jacobs as a journalist. Burnham's ideas came from the history, theory, and practice of architecture; Jacobs's ideas came from observation.

Burnham led the design team for the Plan of Chicago (1909) in a penthouse office atop the Railway Exchange Building (now the Santa Fe Center), with windows overlooking the downtown Loop district. Jane Jacobs's book *The Death and Life of Great American Cities* (1961) was a product of her living on Hudson Street, and walking the sidewalks and streets in New York's Greenwich Village.[48]

> *The best way to plan for downtown is to see how people use it today; to look for its strengths and to exploit and reinforce them.*
> —JANE JACOBS, "DOWNTOWN IS FOR PEOPLE" (1958)[49]

For Jane Jacobs, "the world around here" starts with "the street." She wrote that it "works harder than any other part of downtown. It is the nervous system; it communicates the flavor, the feel, the sights. It is the major point of transaction and communication."[50] The street is a spontaneous stage (plate 8A), with people coming and going, standing aside, moving on, looking at each other, reading the windows, doors, signs, and symbols of the buildings—a gathering place, a civic room.

Jane Jacobs used typically American ways of thinking—empiricism (asking, What is happening?) and pragmatism (asking, Does it fit the street, the block, and the neighborhood?) (plate 8A). She changed the way we imagine the fit of architecture and society.

Architecture and Society

This manifesto recognizes that the relationship between architecture and society is a true dialogue, dynamic and complex.

It starts with questions: Why do we design where we live and work? Why do we not just live in nature, or in chaos? Why does society care about architecture? Why does it really matter?

It answers these questions, by examining architecture itself:

> its origin is nature;
> its task is combining function and expression;
> its legacy is form,

It argues that architecture should be designed to:

fit the purpose;

fit the place;

fit for future possibilities.

The key word is "fit."

notes

1. Nathan Glazer, *From a Cause to a Style* (Princeton, NJ: Princeton University Press, 2007), p. 3.

2. See Nathan Glazer, "What Happened to the Social Agenda?" *American Scholar*, Spring 2007, http://theamericanscholar.org/what-happened-to-the-social-agenda/.

3. Herbert A. Simon, *The Sciences of the Artificial*, 2nd ed. (Cambridge, MA: MIT Press, 1981), p. 129.

4. Clifford Geertz, afterword to *Senses of Place* (Santa Fe, NM: School of American Research Press, 1996), p. 262.

5. Daniel Rodgers, *The Age of Fracture* (Cambridge, MA: Harvard University Press, 2010), p. 5.

6. Miles Glendinning, *Architecture's Evil Empire?* (London: Reaktion Books, 2010), pp. 140, 170.

7. Woody Allen, "If the Impressionists Had Been Dentists," in *Without Feathers* (New York: Random House, 1975), p. 199.

8. Théophile Gautier, preface to *Mademoiselle de Maupin* (Paris, 1934), p. 22. Translated in Iredell Jenkins, "Art for Art's Sake," in *The Dictionary of the History of Ideas*, ed. Philip Wiener (New York: Charles Scribner's Sons, 1968), p. 110.

9. Oscar Wilde, preface to *The Picture of Dorian Gray* (New York: Barnes & Noble Classics, 2003), p. 1.

10. Clive Bell, *Art* (London: Chatto & Windus, 1914), p. 37.

11. Peter Eisenman, quoted in Spiro Kostof, *A History of Architecture: Settings and Rituals*, 2nd ed. (New York: Oxford University Press, 1995), p. 759.

12. Sidney Perkowitz, *Empire of Light: A History of Discovery in Science and Art* (New York: Henry Holt and Company,1996), p. 91.

13. Sara Barrett, "A Master of the Stone Wall Discusses the Perfect Fit," *New York Times*, July 6, 2011.

14. Marc-Antoine Laugier, *Essai sur l'architecture* (1753).

15. Henry D. Thoreau, "Walking," in *Excursions*, ed. Joseph J. Moldenhauer (Princeton, NJ: Princeton University Press, 2007), p. 185.

16. Thomas Jefferson, *Notes on the State of Virginia* (Richmond, VA: J. W. Randolph, 1853), p. 176.

17. Paul Shepard, *Man in the Landscape: A Historic View of the Esthetics of Nature* (New York: Knopf, 1967), chap. 3, "The Image of the Garden," pp. 65–118.

18. Leo Marx, *The Machine in the Garden: Technology and the Pastoral Ideal in America* (New York: Oxford University Press, 1964), p. 3.

19. William Penn, in Samuel Hazard, *Annals of Pennsylvania* (Philadelphia: Hazard and Mitchell, 1850), p. 530.

20. Eugene P. Odum, *Ecology* (New York: Holt, Rinehart and Winston, 1963), chap. 7, "Major Ecosystems of the World," pp. 112–135; quotation from p. 135.

21. Calvert Vaux, *Villas and Cottages: A Series of Designs* (1872; Ann Arbor: University of Michigan Libraries, 2011), p. 111.

22. Ralph Waldo Emerson, *English Traits* (Honolulu, HI: University Press of the Pacific, 2002), p. 41.

23. John Dennis, *Grounds of Criticism in Poetry* (1704), cited in Richard P. Cowl, ed., *The Theory of Poetry in England: Its Development in Doctrines and Ideas from the Sixteenth Century to the Nineteenth Century* (London, Macmillan & Co., 1914), p. 55.

24. Quoted in Charles Edward Gauss, *The Aesthetic Theories of French Artists: 1855 to the Present* (Baltimore, MD: Johns Hopkins University Press, 1949), p. 37.

25. John Dewey, *Art as Experience* (New York: Minton, Balch & Company, 1934), p. 13.

26. Geertz, afterword to *Senses of Place*, p. 262.

27. Claude Lévi-Strauss, *The Savage Mind* (Chicago: University of Chicago Press, 1966), p. 168.

28. Clifford Geertz, *The Interpretation of Cultures* (New York: Basic Books, 1973), p. 45.

29. *The Oxford Companion to Philosophy*, new ed., ed. Ted Honderich (Oxford: Oxford University Press, 2005), s.v. "Franklin, Benjamin."

30. http://www.toronto.ca/planning/urbdesign/civicimprove.htm.

31. Suzanne Langer, *Feeling and Form* (New York: Prentice Hall, 1977).

32. Quoted in Emma Woollacott, "US Plans $1 Billion Moated Embassy," *TG Daily*, February 25, 2010, http://www.tgdaily.com/sustainability-features/48582-us-plans-1-billion-moated-embassy.

33. "LA Officials Unveil $437M Police Headquarters," *Guardian*, October 24, 2009, http://www.guardian.co.uk/world/feedarticle/8772179.

34. John Summerson, *The Classical Language of Architecture* (Cambridge, MA: MIT Press, 1963).

35. Albrecht Dürer, *Of the Just Shaping of Letters* (New York: Dover Publications, 1965), p. 41.

36. Rachel Gershman, "John Chamberlain," The Art Story Foundation, 2012, http://theartstory .org/artist-chamberlain-john.htm.

37. Werner Callebaut and Diego Rasskin-Gutman, *Modularity* (Cambridge, MA: MIT Press, 2005), pp. 283–303.

38. D'Arcy Thompson, *On Growth and Form*, ed. J. T. Bonner (Cambridge: Cambridge University Press, 1961).

39. E. H. Gombrich, *The Sense of Order* (Ithaca, NY: Cornell University Press, 1979), pp. 164–165.

40. Ibid., p. 165.

41. Ibid., p. 9.

42. Horatio Greenough, *Form and Function: Remarks on Art, Design, and Architecture* (Berkeley: University of California Press, 1947), p. 71.

43. Glazer, *From a Cause to a Style*, p. 278.

44. Claude Lévi-Strauss, *A World on the Wane*, trans. John Russell (New York: Criterion Books, 1961), p. 127.

45. Henry Taylor Blake, *Chronicles of New Haven Green from 1638 to 1862* (New Haven, CT: Tuttle, Morehouse & Taylor, 1898), p. 10.

46. Quoted in Thomas S. Hines, "Architecture: The City Beautiful Movement," in *Encyclopedia of Chicago*, http://encyclopedia.chicago history.org/pages/61.html.

47. William H. Whyte, *The Social Life of Small Urban Spaces* (Washington, DC: Conservation Foundation, 1980).

48. Jane Jacobs, *The Death and Life of Great American Cities* (New York: Random House, 1961).

49. Jane Jacobs, "Downtown Is for People," in *The Exploding Metropolis*, ed. William H. Whyte (Berkeley: University of California Press, 1993), p. 160.

50. Ibid.

index